MEMORY TRICKS

MEMORY TRICKS

Zev Shanken

FCP

Full Court Press
Englewood Cliffs, New Jersey

Published in the United States of America
by Full Court Press, 601 Palisade Avenue,
Englewood Cliffs, NJ 07632
fullcourtpressnj.com

ISBN 978-1-938812-78-1
Library of Congress Catalog No. 2016947596

Book design by Barry Sheinkopf for Bookshapers (bookshapers.com)

Copy editing by Cindy Hochman of 100 Proof Copyediting Services

Cover art by the author

Colophon by Liz Sedlack

To

Alice, Mike, Rim, Jay, and Jackie.
Here are the drafts I'm offering strangers.

Special thanks to Alice Twombly, Stephen Bluestone, and Cindy Hochman for advice in helping me prepare this manuscript. Gratitude to *brevitas*, an online poetry group devoted to the short poem, with whom I shared a number of these poems in earlier drafts.

ACKNOWLEDGMENTS

"Outward Bound" as "Elegy for Norman Mailer," *Jewish Standard* (2007)

"A Nice Day," *Jewish Currents Calendar* (2015)

"When the Father of an Old Girlfriend Dies," *Pooled Ink* (2015)

"Two Schools" as "Two Yeshivas," *Menorah* (1989)

"St. Anselm at Yad V'shem," *Weathered Pages: The Poetry Pole*, Blue Begonia
     Press, Yakima, WA (2005)

"Special Education," *Yes, Poetry* (July 2012)

"My Mother's Martin Luther King Day," *Brownstone Anthology* (2012)

"High Noon," *The New Verse News* (December 2015)

"Mother at 90," *Jewish Rites of Death: Stories of Beauty and Transformation*,
     Terra Nova Books, Santa Fe, NM (2016)

"Boxcars," *Al Het*, Blue Begonia Press (1996)

"The Razbash and Others on Judgment," *Jewish Currents* (2015)

CONTENTS

Lost Watch

❧

And How Old Are You?

❧

Collateral Damage

❧

A Cool Drink in the Middle of the Night

❧

Happy Morning After

❧

Tales of The Razbash

❧

Lost Watch

First Symphony

Sometimes a symphony over the radio can make the air I inhaled
through the open window of my father's car one hot July afternoon,
driving through Chinatown from my new wife and new apartment,

come back.

I banged the dashboard whistling Mahler's First Symphony,
held the wheel with my knees, made Mahler black, Israeli, Spanish, French, be-bop,
rock, then back to first song.

I had pulled it off, gotten out alive, college degree years late, so what?
I would teach or something. I parked the car and
raced to Shakespeare Seminar, Mahler and new wife on my mind.

Newlyweds

Sliding the potatoes into sparkling sautéed onions,
we joked about the hard Scotch tape
that kept your mother's cookbook together.

When you announced that you had figured out
when to add the basil leaves,
your voice blended perfectly with laughter down the hall.

The whole apartment smelled of plastic shower curtain,
a wedding gift from my mother's favorite cousin.
Every evening after work, every recipe made sense.

Our Faces

Our faces resemble genetic misprints of our faces in 1969.
The young technicians in the sky had miscopied the markers,
not yet understanding what it meant to read code.
They tried to be good interns but never listened well.
Even when it really mattered, never listened well.
This took a toll on our DNA, a new word in 1969.

Birthday Poem

Our Living Creature is the same as always,
but the atoms that run our clunky train
have recently started to grumble.
Because we are human, we know what will come,
but the Living Creature is a puppy dog.

Dear Fido:

This makes no sense to you,
for your job is to not understand,
but may we request, when the molecules kvetch,
you not yelp from the back of the car?
Our atoms have a God-given right to be free,
but we will be with you to the end of the line.
We promise.

Airbnb, Spain

I see creamy blue bedroom walls,
buttery blue-pink morning sky,
caramel-blue dog shit below the balcony
on blue and light-blue orange tiles.
Picasso was a realist.

I hear a snoring wife, air conditioners,
then the clunk of the Keurig and a rattle of pills.
Instead of taking a sunrise swim,
I wait for her to tell me how she slept.
I, too, am a realist.

Rugby Live in a Dublin Pub

That little boys dream of becoming great
in a sport you do not understand
with skills you watch in ignorance
and rules you've never argued—

That everyone here will see these plays
as metaphors to teach their sons,
as rituals you never mocked
your mother for not knowing—

If you note this in a foreign land, my friend,
you've reached first base in the tourist game.

Mountain Lodge, Italy

Lost

Lost luggage, lost record of reservations,
Yet so many fewer fat people than in Newark.

Café

Same price for big or small pizza?
Yes, same amount of ingredients.

Holiday Lodge Waitress

To have a smile like hers that says,
"My brain is a vagina.
Enter me, enter me, wonderful world.
You are making me so smart!"

Museum

Man the bowl maker, man the mistake maker,
the ready to forgive, the warrior.

Little Mountain Ranges

Those little mountain ranges of tightly wrinkled skin
drying inside my thighs and underneath my arms,
I find on you as well.

So life is not as unfair as we had feared,
or at least not as lonely,
which is almost the same thing.

Let's think of the wrinkles as sheets of silk
that ancient merchants, scaling mountains,
devoted their lives to deliver.

Dirty Laundry

We visit a woman I loved fifty years ago.
I introduce my wife to her husband.
We exchange photo albums.
How sweet to have come this far.

The same scent of trusting arms.
A photo of her bedroom. *Her blood on my fingers,*
so much hotter than the wetness we knew
when we practiced everything but.

A photo of Jonathan. "Here was my first love."
"I thought I was your first love."
"You were my first lust; he was my first love."

We help her move her wrought-iron table
to make room to serve us vegan quiche.
Screeches of her bed frame on the tiles.
Firmly, slowly, she presses her head on the wall.
"All I wanted was to stay virgin till I got married."

Later, in the car, my wife observes
that if we consolidate our dirty laundry into one valise,
we could avoid the cost of extra baggage on the flight home.

Hard Questions

Let's put our marriage up for adoption.
Why deprive others of a happy home
just because it may no longer meet our needs?

Let's put our parents up for adoption.
Why let their needs go unsatisfied
just because they have self-centered kids?

Let's put our private lives up for adoption.
Why deprive others of our life as art
just because we don't mean it?

Getting It

It's not this in and of itself
but what caused this.
It's not 'A' but 'A prime.'
The real problem only looks like this
and if I were really sensitive
I would understand the difference between
this and this prime.

The battle itself proves I've lost,
and why do I see it as a battle?
Her very point.
I tear a candy wrapper open with my teeth.
She wins again.

Lost Watch

What if I find my watch
where I am sure I left it,
but not where it really is?

Falling asleep, I remember
where it really is.
Do I wake my wife to tell her?

Outward Bound

I climbed a post higher than a roof,
stood on its top, and leaped to ring a bell.
I had choked halfway up.
Colleagues shouted encouragement.
I summoned Norman Mailer,
stabbed my wife, sodomized the maid,
walked the parapet of my father-in-law's
American Dream penthouse,
and rang the goddamn bell.
Cheers from below.
When I reported this triumph
to my wife of 30 years,
she replied with this question:
"And how old are you?"

JFK

1.

"What would President Kennedy say?"
I used to ask myself
when tempted to sexually misbehave.
O! Ellen Welles, I could have kissed you more.

2.

From my window I saw a man
rest his forearm on a street lamp
to cover his eyes.
He was on his way home.
Kennedy had been shot.
I'm sure that's why he was crying.

3.

His press conference photo—
the one on the cover of *The Kennedy Wit*,
his famous smile and simultaneous pointing
to the next admiring victim.
I was looking at the cover just the other day
while taking down our bedroom bookcase
for my wife's new office.
I said to her, "His capped front teeth.
We didn't notice those things then."

Is There a Word for It?

Is there a word for the feeling you get
when you skim pages in a book
you enjoyed reading in college—
when you find something new
in the parts you underlined?
Whatever the word, I know it
when I hear you say a word
the way you said it when we met.
It's the way you wear your hat.

Nostalgia

If I had known how good it was back then,
I would never have left.
What a fool I was to let time pass!
What was I thinking?
I should have stayed in 1964 the same way
I should have stayed at NYU
the same way I should have stopped
the breakup of the Beatles.

And How Old Are You?

Construction Site

When I took him to construction sites,
I loved the way he reveled in the joy of force
without ego or revenge. Thirty years later
I understand he was the construction site.

A Wise Roman Haircut

His mother and I try sarcasm. "You got it good, Son.
She's giving you the best years of her life, and
you're getting away with it on racist grounds.
You're taking advantage, and you know what?
You're lying to yourself too, because you are in love with her."

He sneers.

"You have a convenient misunderstanding
that you two will never get married
because she's not Jewish, but be honest, Son,
do you really believe she's visiting Israel
purely out of intellectual curiosity?"

Nervous laugh.

I press my advantage:
"You're flying with a dishonest safety net."
He asks, "Yeah, but didn't you ever date a non-Jew?"
I answer, "This is not about me"
and write this letter in my mind.

Dear Suzanne,
This evening I remember how we would audit
Salzman's graduate course on Jewish self-hatred
and then race to your dorm to make love till dawn
after I held forth about Zionist ideologies
that you told me you'd explain to your Southern Belle mother.

Today I went to a hairstylist, first time in twenty years. I said,
"Give me that austere Roman cut that emperors have on statues—
Don't hide the bald spot. Use it to my advantage."

Sick Call

"What did you tell him?"
She asks the father
after his visit to their son.

"I made it so he'll never be cured.
I told him it was just a stage
that even I went through."

For Our Graduates

1.
I love to hear you laugh out loud
at sitcom reruns
you missed over the past four years.

2.
Remember the difference between Daedalus and Icarus.
Daedalus built his own maze. Therefore he devised an escape.
Poor Icarus, however, trapped in his father's maze,
tried his father's wings to get out.
It was logical. His father even encouraged it.
Those who criticize Icarus for flying too near the sun are unfair.
His mistake was he used his father's wings.

3.
May you never have to learn
how smart you have to be
to understand your dreams.

Teaching *The Odyssey* After *Death of a Salesman*

When my high school students learn that Odysseus sleeps with Circe,
they accuse him of being another Willy Loman, guilty of sleeping around.
Like a chorus of pandering summer camp prigs,
they chant against philandering bums.

"If it's wrong for Willy Loman to cheat on his wife,
then it's wrong for Odysseus as well!"

"But Odysseus only does it to trick the witch," I protest,
"into freeing the men she had turned into pigs."
Don't these sanctimonious brats see the point
is that Odysseus does return to his wife?

"If it's wrong for Willy Loman to cheat on his wife,
then it's wrong for Odysseus as well!"

With the casuistry of a mad Talmudic sage, I defend Odysseus,
hero of the Hellenists my ancestors despised.
With embarrassing intensity, I praise the Greeks,
like a salesman who does not know himself.

St. Anselm at Yad V'Shem

I tell my students at Yad V'Shem that God is a metaphor
for the power of goodness.
It can feel like it moves mountains.
It can feel like it began the world.
It can feel like it gives strength to the weary,
sight to the blind, pride to the lowly,
lessons to the proud, splendor to all that exists.
It can feel like the force that makes every star burn
is the same as the force that wants you to be kind.

But it's only a metaphor?
Yes, but can you think of a greater metaphor?
The students are silent.
Then Jeff says, "That's really good."
Later I learn he lost his mother on 9/11.

Kali in the Faculty Photocopying Room

While the new teacher's copies of Cavafy's "Ithaka"
clunk onto the tray, I ask if she knows that "Ithaka"
was Jackie Onassis's favorite poem, read at her funeral.
She hadn't known. She will tell her students.
"If they know who Jackie Kennedy was," says another, in line.
I add that, re-reading the poem last year, I decided that
Ithaka was a gay man's thoughts on the vagina.
The new teacher goes all relative on me. I elaborate.

"It's the letter of a *mensch* to his young gay lovers,
advising they not disparage the gems of civilization
when they learn its conventional prize is no prize at all."
She puts copies of "Ithaka" in her 'First Lesson' folder,
says "Goodbye, nice meeting you," and does not smile
when I tell her I know her name means 'beautiful' in Greek.

Among Schoolchildren

Acting Normal

Sometimes when I act normal, I imagine my parents watching me
in a new neighborhood. Father belittles Mother's protective lingering
by praising a repartee he overheard me say last week
to a kid twice my age down the street.

Museum

Before a tour of the Whitney Museum,
I take my inner-city students to a diner on Madison Avenue.
I ask them why they giggled triumphantly after placing their orders.
That ignorant server didn't first take our money.

Sheet Music

The photographs of 1930s bandleaders.
Change the hair, jacket, bow tie, chin, and teeth.
Make the glasses new. Nobody looks like that anymore,
even if you correct for fashion.

Special Education

New lovers make the mistake of new teachers.
To allay anxiety, they smile,
tell their student who can't do long division,
"It's easy. Nothing to it.
Watch me. Here's the trick."

If it were easy for me, Teacher,
I wouldn't be here.
If you tell me there's nothing to it,
we don't belong together.

High Noon

1.

Then the good guy reaches for his hidden gun,
cries, "Take that, you wicked terrorists!"
After the commercial, he kills them all,
speaks modestly on the Evening News
about just doing his job as a citizen.

2.

Gary Cooper's new wife threatens
to leave him if he breaks his promise
and goes after Frank Miller. Coop says,
"Seems I gotta do this." Loads his gun.
She leaves but, when she hears shots,
runs back and shoots a bad guy herself.

3.

A student I don't know walks into my class,
shouts an obscenity, turns and runs.
I give chase. Three flights down the stairs,
he stops, out of breath. I ask him his name.
No answer. I ask for his ID. No answer.
I demand that he come with me to the dean.
He doesn't move. The brat is damn lucky
I left my gun at the ranch.

Muffin

I am practically old.
I dream of movie stars protectively, not as secrets to be tried.
I know the dangers of a frozen lake.
At last the sixties have become a blur.
I spend my genius on acting normal.
I have a healthy suspicion of fancy high tech.
I look at a parting cloud and see a parting cloud.

So tell me why I felt so cold
when my old cat died.
Her open mouth, a round rake,
a piercing mound of sturdy fur.
The room's air oddly formal,
Muffin's presence, a diminishing speck.
I stared at her daybed and bowed.

Day Camp Bus

Waiting with my son for his first day camp bus,
we eat his favorite maple-dripping waffles
and write a poem about a runaway rocket
that wanted to be a day camp bus.
We joke about listening to the counselors.
Last week he forgot to show us
a note from his teacher about behavior.
After we punished him, I heard him say to the cat,
"I'll always be bad in school."
Now he tells me to go away.
He doesn't want the other kids seeing him with his father.
I tell him I'm just a man sitting on the steps.
No one will know who I am.
"Yeah, right," he says. "Just a working man
enjoying a simple cup of coffee on his break."
We're friends again.
And when the bus arrives I say to myself,
"I really considered giving this up
just to find meaning in life?"

Two Schools

I was new to the school and cried all the way home.
I was not used to Hebrew-in-Hebrew Labor Zionist, Bronx.
The next day my father spoke to the teacher.
For weeks Aviva didn't call on me but
put me in study groups with the smart boys and girls.
I still remember the first answer I volunteered.

When we moved again, I cried all the way home.
I was not used to Yiddishized English, Elizabeth, New Jersey.
The next day my father spoke to the teacher.
For an hour he didn't call on me, but
when the boys broke up into small study groups,
Rabbi Goldberg invited me for a private walk down the hall.
"This will be your class as per now."
It was a class of boys two grades below mine.

Now, as a teacher, I remember these schools
whenever a new child joins my class,
and whenever there's an election in Israel.

Collateral Damage

Why My Father Became a Rabbi

He was stationed in North Africa,
fasting at the makeshift synagogue on Yom Kippur,
when he learned he was scheduled for a mission.
Boarding his B-25, he asked Tail Gunner McGuire
for a cup of black coffee. The captain protested,
"Don't break your fast now. Bad luck for us all."

It was a low-flying mission to bomb German troops.
"That low, they can shoot you down with a rifle," he used to add.
My father prayed that he not be off-target,
lest he hit the American troops on the other side of the line.
When the photographs came back,
he learned that every bomb had been true.
And that's why he became a rabbi.

Alexander the Great

I am ten, riding home with my father from Radio City Music Hall
after seeing *Alexander the Great*.
He asks me what I thought of the movie.
I throw the popcorn on the dashboard and grab my throat.
In a clipped Richard Burton accent I gasp,
"I leave my kingdom to the strongest."
He opens the window a crack to let his cigarette smoke escape.
"Your father almost lost his life stopping a modern-day Alexander the Great."

Collateral Damage

1.

Dressed proudly in his First Lieutenant uniform,
my father, with his bombing crew on leave,
climbed over the rubble of Catania,
when a ten-year old,
resting on a homemade crutch,
pointed directly at him and said,
"Tu boom-boom Catania."
One wound and 54 missions later,
recovering from battle fatigue,
my father returned to Catania for rehab.
The rubble had been cleared away.

After the war, as a young rabbi,
whenever he needed a motivational sermon,
my mother would suggest that he "bomb Catania."
When he told the congregation of the boy's rebuke
and of the tenacious Catanians' recovery,
he would stroke his nose,
his way of holding back in public.
Nobody knew this but us.
Twenty years later, they divorced.

2.

I tell the war but not the rabbi part of the story
when I teach my students to be resilient,
when I read of purely surgical aerial strikes,

when I see children suffer grown-up madness,
and when, at the Seder, we read that God rebuked the angels
for cheering when Pharaoh's armies drowned.
But during the meal, when the gossip turns to couples,
perfect for each other, splitting,
I remember the rabbi part of the story.
Nobody saw it coming.

After My Father's Surgery

I look at the joke books, beside his bed, that his stepchildren sent,
but I remember the Hist-o-map that hung on his study wall,
graphically displaying the development of civilizations up to 1958.
He tells me of a boyhood friend who told him it's easy to ignore pain.
"So I tried it and it's worked ever since.
We used it in St. Louis, Chicago, San Antonio, the Army...ever since."
I don't ask who he means by "we."

I remember a family legend that at five he bragged he could ride a bike.
When challenged, he rode the bike perfectly. He did not fall.
Was it that boyhood friend who moved him to bluff so well?
But it wasn't a bluff: he rode the bike perfectly.
So the legend goes.

Last night they put him on a morphine drip.
He asks me what the nurses are doing.

Boxcars

To boxcar hobo angelic hipster
open American hero poems
howled after World War II,
I slipped this note into a railroad car
in a San Francisco stockyard:
 "Whoever you are, I love you."

Then I recalled I had first heard that line
from my father in a story of the War.
 "Whoever you are, I love you"
read the note of cremated Jewish girl
found in her journal after World War II.

Whoever you are, I love you
now for picturing me in heaven
with Kerouac and smoke,
looking down on myself, posturing,
imagining postwar Zen poet railroad cars
instead of boxcars for the Jews.

Whoever you are, I thank you.
Whenever I pose, I'm betrayed.

For My Kid Sister

When you were in Israel for the second time,
I used to remember you, in synagogue,
deliberately misreading an ancient text
to divine new meaning in coincidence.

Now you're back, working with people
who never read those books that made
our lives make sense. But I still imagine you
in Israel, doing a Rashi on Basho,

the sedre, and Persian astrology,
devising puns in languages nobody speaks,
but somehow still convincing me
that hungry sleepy morning prayers

really matter in a way,
and that knowing resembles nothing at all.

My Mother's Martin Luther King Day

—Laredo, Texas, January 2009

Dr. Gutierrez tells me he's surprised my mother has lasted this long.
Her arteries are blocked. Her ears, eyes, digestion, and brain
are starved of blood. Little veins are pitching in,
but they will soon wear out.
There are operations for this, but her body is too frail.
He tells me my mother has had a good life. Her caregivers love her.
She is clean and dry. She has helped many people.
Her students loved her. He looks at my eyes.
"I'd hug you if I wasn't sick myself."

Later, Mother asks that we look at the three photo albums
she won in the divorce.
Laredo from birth through World War II,
the Northeast as a rabbi's wife till 1979,
Laredo again for 30 years.
She doesn't recognize the Jewish boys at the Laredo Air Corps Base.
She doesn't remember me thin, and insists I never wore a mustache.
Who's that rabbi receiving a Man of the Year Award for being a Freedom Rid
And here's the room we're in right now when the furniture was new.
"I've been here a long time."
We watch the Martin Luther King celebrations on TV.
Mother asks, "What did Martin Luther King do?"
She wants to have her eyes fixed;
the pleasures she used to get from reading in bed.
"Just twenty minutes or so before going to sleep. It was so enjoyable."

Memory Tricks

I remember my mother's memory tricks.
Rhythmic: Eight and five are *thir*teen; seven and five are *twelve*.
Ironic: Four times your age equals my age.
Pun: The Hebrew word for 'only' is '*rahq.*' It's *only* a *rock.*

Now she can't remember her nurse's name.
I try: She is tall, like a hill. *Hil*da. But everybody's tall.
Nor can she remember the name of her current bodily affliction.
I try: It hurts your *tushie* like a *ham*mer, but *Roy* Rogers will fix it.
Hammer+Roy = hemorrhoids, get it?
Blank stare. As I explain the ridiculous connection,
we both start laughing so hard that I feel my heart beating in my ears.
I wheel her to the Sabbath table. "Let's make Kiddush."
Her lips coach me from her wheelchair. I know all the words by heart.

Mother at Ninety

1.

The nurse explains in Spanish how her other patients are much worse.
I glance at Mother, *kvelling* at my Spanish from her wheelchair.
After she leaves, Mother whispers to me,
"I think she has a crush on you."

2.

The nurse and I help Mother find a word.
We bend over her wheelchair, calling out words as in charades.
Mother shakes her head and starts to cry.
"Everybody's trying to be nice to me and all I do is complain!"

3.

Her sisters, children, and grandchildren sing
"Happy Birthday," and help her blow out the candles.
While she eats her cake, we play
"Our Favorite Thing About Mother."
She smiles, periodically asking for clarifications.
After the party, I wheel her into her room.
We kiss goodnight. Then she calls me back and says,
"You have such nice friends."

My Sister's Glasses

Dr. Gutierrez demonstrates Mother's dependence on the breathing tube.
The staff uses the word "coded" as if everyone knows what it means.
A nurse spreads Mother's eyelids apart. Her eyes are coated gray.
I am told they withdrew her feeding tube to prevent overtaxing her heart.
"Yet her feet," the doctor adds, "are uncharacteristically robust."

They point to machines, present options. More than once the doctor says,
"There is no hurry." I recall that, twenty years ago, Mother
drove to San Antonio to visit Sophie, dying of cancer.
Mother phoned me that night. "Don't ever let me get that way."
But Sophie was in pain. Mother is dry, clean, unaware.
My sister and I make a decision, check off boxes, sign forms.

Then my sister shows me that the hinges of her glasses are loose.
The lenses keep falling out. I ask the doctor if he knows where in Laredo
I can get eyeglass frames repaired on short notice.
I leave my sister with my mother and drive across town.
"Is your sister a client of ours?" the receptionist asks.
"No, this is an emergency." I gladly move to the end of the line.

A Cool Drink
in the Middle of the Night

❧

Culling My Books

The ones I've read and loved—
they are not people.
Free the space.

The ones I ought to read some day—
they are people and I am a grown-up.
Free the space.

The ones I loved at first sight—
after 30 years or pages still love at first sight.
Free the space.

And the ones that changed my life?
Change my shelf, free more than space,
make me free at last.

Casablanca at Seventy

The movie world gave us courage
to live in a desert we loved for its waters
and claim we were misinformed.

Someday we will understand this.
When that plane leaves the ground
and we're not on it
we'll regret it for the rest of our lives.

Yet brave and serene as a hill of beans,
we fix the casino we call the *real world*
and fight our second world's war,
shocked, shocked.

When We All Took Drugs

When we all took drugs we took them to escape
our true selves I mean into our true selves

When we all took drugs our only problem was
others did not take drugs I mean the same drugs

When we all took drugs we understood the horror
of needing medicine to be normal I mean to be normal

Zayde

Mother means *young*.
It once meant *mature*.

Wife means *wife*.
It once meant *trapped*.

Doing okay is depressing.
It whispers, *You could have been great*.

You ask Freddy the Fish
What's going on up there?

He answers, *Life*.
We all visit it once.

It's not bad, but
you gotta do your own cooking.

From a Warm Car,
Parked on a Cold Busy Street

That man who waits unmoved for the light
must have been beaten as a kid.
I wish my folks had toughened me up.

That *hasid* who strides full force past the bus
does not hail a cab. Business? Medical needs?
Looking for a synagogue before it's too late?

That homeless guy waddles in an autumn jacket—
poor man or poorly raised? Poor guy.
I should take them all in. I have room,

but would be misunderstood,
especially by that pretty one with stiff blonde hair.
Here comes a shivering meter maid.

Leaves

Those leaves whose tenacity we loved last November
have fallen like all the rest.
They did not have willpower after all.
But we knew this then. Leaves have no will.
It was just a passing metaphor.
Yet some leaves do linger longer than others,
and others fall without a fight.
Of course, it's not really a fight.

Chronic Back Pain

He is the pockmarked sleepover cousin
Mother promised you an erector set
for being nice to, but you misunderstood.

He borrows your toothbrush. He brags that he knows
the pattern of your bathroom tiles by heart.
You test him. He's right. He asks,
'Are you asleep yet? Am I your best friend?'

He uses words you thought you knew,
but you can't reach for the dictionary.
He's never cautious about advice.
After all, you won't die if he's wrong,
and if he's right: *Post hoc ergo propter hoc.*

If he's not your best friend,
why do you talk about him all the time?

You Must Change Your Life

When they told me I'd lose muscle mass,
I thought my biceps, not my ass.

When they warned me that my heart would tire,
I thought mechanics, not desire.

I never understood my brain
would turn as unreliable as rain.

I never had to change my life;
my body did it for me.

Time Is a House

Time is a house with wiring from a basement fuse box accessible
through the trap door made of the same paneling as the walls
like the secret passages in *Clue* that we taught both kids in the basement
before we hired Phyllis and her second husband, Herman, to renovate
when our twenty-six-year old daughter was twelve.

Three weeks ago Misha and I visited the bench on Riverside Park that
Herman used to sit and read on until his cancer made sitting painful and
reading, we imagined, impossible. We read out loud the plaque Phyllis
had installed and agreed to donate to keep the park fit for the future.

What Misha Knew

Misha didn't know
what I was doing
with my iPhone

when I put my head
next to his,
stretched my left arm

toward the Lincoln Center fountain
to take a selfie.
"A what?"

"Our picture to send our wives."
"I went to school here
when it was a vocational school

before they tore it down
for the upper ten percent
in 1955."

A Nice Day

On a day like this, I don't want sex
to thrill me, revive my soul, make me
feel young. I want sex a normal, natural
meal, whose main course is standard fare,
a novel whose plot is not what counts,
where *a wasted life* is an oxymoron,
and nothing means two things at once.

A friend writes, all my metaphors are sex;
another, that I'm always teaching;
a third tells me I'm too Jewish, and tells me
an old Jewish joke. There are three ages:
young, old, and *you look great.* I love my friends
who know me and the ones who get me wrong.
Getting a friend wrong? Another oxymoron.

Happy Morning After

To Good Old Sex

You always knew more than I, even with strangers.
You were patient, but was there a choice?
You made the home full when unemployment
and misdirected anger threatened to destroy it.

Unlike food, your excess made me thin.
Unlike sleep, your promise made me fly.
Unlike wine, you made my vision clear.
Unlike love, you worshipped only greed.

I owe you so much, dear friend, dear constant, secret conversation.
May I wheel you through the garden? Is the staff treating you well?
Do they bring you a cool drink in the middle of the night?

Ghosts

1.

When we made love,
you loved all the men you had ever loved
and wanted to love and never thought of loving—
and floated, curled, and disappeared
and then came back to fetch me.
I loved waiting until we tasted related,
until normal words seemed slightly misspelled,
until I wished I were a woman so I could say,
"I want to carry your child for nine thousand months."

2.

When I was in love with your face,
I loved every woman's face,
not as a lover, but as a poet,
and easily understood the difference.
When I think of you now,
you're a dream without a plot,
a presence without a storyline,
the girl with the funny last name in Algebra II,
who must be a grandmother by now.

3.

You were the perfect wife and the married mistress
who whispers, "It's wrong, I know it's wrong."
Except you would whisper, "You have no idea,"
and I was always too thoughtful to ask
if you meant your pleasure,
or that overthinking had made me blind.

When the Father of an Old Girlfriend Dies

If I had married her, I would be ordering food
and helping her make a life abstract for the rabbi.
She and I would be calculating Frequent Flyer Miles
and how to write an obituary without sounding trite.
I would be among the first to pick up the shovel.

But many years ago I did not marry that woman,
so my day is filled with absence of loss.
I will not have to ask if it is appropriate to speak publicly
about the time she warned me that he would suck me into an argument
over the value of monogamy in a post-modern world.

Ties as binding as blood were not severed today.
That man she is going to bury—I never danced with him.

Freshman Year

With tender gratitude, he says to the hooker,
"Let me kiss you on the lips."
She replies like a brat, like a lamb,
like a shrink, like a friend,
"I give blowjobs all day. Are you sure
you want to kiss this mouth?"

Back in the dorm his roommate asks,
"Do you people believe in heaven and hell?"
"You mean," he asks, "after you die?"

Doctor Zhivago

I still love that we could never remember
if it was Zhivago or Lara who answered,
"If we keep wondering we should go mad,"
when asked if they would have been lovers
had they met 20 years before.

Secret Lovers League

They send out signals only members can decipher.
They know it is not like marriage or work,
or the deeds their children will remember them by.
They know being remembered isn't everything.

They walk through old church cemeteries
to read the names of women and men,
born the same year, without the same last name.
They kneel and whisper to the grass, "Welcome
to the Secret Lovers League."

Love Games

Shooting Craps
The rules are hard to get straight.
Just playing is a victory.

Backgammon
We play the back game because we have bad dice.
We feel brave and smart, and have no other choice.

Chess
We follow set patterns until real life intervenes.
But we don't explain it like that.

Checkers
My end is your home. I become a king.
The same is true on your end. Now we get to go backwards.

Scrabble
Great words don't always fit on the board.
Whose board?

Stretch, Twitch, Itch

Stretch

The episiotomy to mitigate the stretch and tear of birth
The endearing stretch of a one-syllable name when "Happy Birthday" is sung
The stretch of Asian currencies or Scottish words for *lover* in a creative family
   Scrabble game
The stretched point of a spurious argument to avert a daughter's suspension
The bathing suit stretched to expose; the pants waist stretched to conceal
The strenuous stretch the sensei demands charging his trainees to obey
The reverent stretch the yogi displays coaxing her disciples to focus
The saxophone solo stretches the margarita's crisp rim
   until its empty glass and grains of luminous salt alter the image
   of the things you love
   and you remember that glass comes from liquefied sand,
   heated and skillfully stretched
The last stretch of the cat or race or your arms before going to bed

Twitch

Crawling in the kitchen—dinner, radiators, the radio, linoleum—
he twitches until he is safe—

The first rush of nicotine—his damp fingers twitch in smoke—

"You know, you have an involuntary tic under your left eye."
"It's not involuntary. But it feels so good."

er revealing that he smiles broadly to cover his facial twitch,
adds that he feels like he's just walked naked with strangers.
week later he is fired.

e professional gambler figures it out—his opponent's twitch is not a tell,
t the way he is—

e smart-ass student asks him why he twitches—like this—with his face.

re-emptive strike—at randomness—It is not only the face—

Itch

itch to grab the bat from a son afraid of the ball
itch of chalk in the back of your nose on back-to-school night each time
itch of overused running shoes, copy machine chemicals, new books
itch to touch her hair again—you will always know this about her
itch in your lung as spiritual as smell
itch you choose to call wisdom, and sleep

This Poem

This poem does not exist
to get published or its poet laid
or sell a product creatively
or win a famous prize.

This poem does not exist
to comfort mourners or advance a cause
or get a mayor to fix a street
or fit a song or ape a style.

This poem does not exist
to please a lover or a wife
or sublimate a dirty need
or help a child sleep.

This poem does not exist.

Intake

After conferences scripted like Miranda recitations,
patient advocates proud to say her name right,
chaplains clarifying in-house feuds,
and brochures of cartoons defending the tubes in her arm,

she hears muffled News and Weather from a distant radio,
looks at the wrapper of a thousand-year-old snack,
waits for her anesthesiologist,
and recalls with religious intensity last winter's dull afternoon.

What's the Best Disease for a Poet?

I used to think the best disease was cancer,
 because I would know not to waste time.
But then I thought of the pain and pain pills
 that would poison my mind too much to concentrate.
So I thought a heart condition would do the trick,
 because I wouldn't waste energy.
But the fear of getting upset would poison my will
 too much to dare something new.
Maybe arthritis? I wouldn't waste words,
 because every word would jolt my thumbs with pain.
But I don't write in longhand anymore,
 and keyboarding doesn't hurt enough to teach concision.
So now I think the best disease is obesity.
 It would make me sluggish enough to sit still.
Moreover, overeating would keep me up all night,
 so I could edit, revise, and have another
ice-cream sundae while reflecting on how every calorie counts,
 but never counts forever.
It would also make me a better proofreader than if I had OCD,
 where I would waste all night
troubled that the word *daughter* has two syllables,
 while the word *son* has only one.

Happy Morning After

Watering the Plants

The problem with love: it's normal and not.
All plants turn air and light into life, ho-hum.

Buttons on a Mattress

I can't stop remembering when you read to me that time
or space or something is a ball bearing rolling on a taut balloon.

Breakfast

The curls on the coast of a slow-cooking omelet.

Tales of The Razbash

The Razbash is an acronym for Rabbi Zev ben Shlomo, an imaginary friend in the poet's childhood and alter ego throughout his adult life. The word "ben" is Hebrew for "son of."

The Razbash and Other Rabbis on Judgment

Rabbi Moshe used to say, *Judge others in these three ways:*
How they report their 9/11 memories,
how they behave in an argument,
and how they pronounce foreign words.

Rabbi Aaron added,
How they correct those who mispronounce foreign words.
Rabbi Joshua added,
How they explain their children's choice of college and a friend's divorce.

Rabbi Shmuel used to say,
Judge others by how early they leave for work,
how early they leave work,
and how they stand at prayer.
Rabbi Dovid added,
How they recall a childhood toy without disparaging a sibling.
Rabbi Shlomo added,
How many times they press an elevator button.

Every morning The Razbash would say to his students,
Look at trees as if they are judging you.
Then he would add,
But they are not judging you.

The Test of Judaism

"God tested Abraham and said to him. . . 'Take your son ... and offer him ... as a burnt offering ...' So Abraham rose early in the morning."

— Gen. 22:2

The Razbash asks, "Why did Abraham not question God's commandment to sacrifice his son?" Then The Razbash answers his question, saying, "Actually, Abraham did question. Here is the unrecorded exchange."

"Here I am, Oh Lord,

dagger in hand, poised to follow your instructions with zeal.

But I must have answers, lest I disobey.

Do I burn Isaac naked or with clothes?

Do I sprinkle, drain, pour, or throw his blood on the pyre?

Do I burn him up completely or share him with my family?

Does hair count as fur?

Now, since the place you have shown me is the future Temple Mount,

should I sweep the ashes into the future Dung Gate,

as is instructed for an *olah* sacrifice?"

"Abraham, Abraham," God says. "Do not sacrifice your son.

For now I see how seriously you take Judaism."

Mystery of Joseph Solved

"His brothers were jealous of him, but his father kept the matter in mind."

— *Gen. 37:11*

*e Razbash asks, "Why did Joseph never let his father know that he was alive
d prospering in Egypt? Because Joseph believed that his father was in on the
ot. Here are Joseph's thoughts after his brothers threw him into the pit to die."*

hy did Father send me here?
esn't he know my brothers hate me for winning
at coat of many colors he gave me for snitching?
d what did he mean when he ordered me to
o and see if all is well with your brothers
d with the flocks, and bring word back to me."
hy didn't he, at least, send me with provisions for them,
Jesse does with David for his brothers in the field?
cause that would have concealed Father's real intent.
ther sent me to spy on them, knowing exactly what they would do.

ther must be in on this! Yes,
en I reported my second dream—
t Father, too, would bow down to me
e the stars and the moon and the sun in the sky—
rebuked me in public for the first time.
at was the signal to my brothers.
at night they went to Father's tent.
d become dangerous—not only would I usurp them,

but I had Father in my dreams as well.

"Yes," Father thought. "This dreamer of dreams,
this favored son of my old age,
will outsmart me as I outsmarted my father
to steal the blessing meant for my brother."
So with my brothers, Father plotted this plan,
admonishing them as they left his tent,
"This meeting never took place."

If I ever get out of this pit alive,
I swear before God I will hide from my father
until I am certain he cannot collude
with my brothers against me again.

Morning Prayer

Every morning after washing, the Razbash recited the following prayer:

May I find pleasure in pretending that the present moment matters.
May I find wisdom in remembering that the present moment matters.

Love Your Neighbor as Yourself

"…you shall love your neighbor as yourself"
—Lev. 19:17

The Razbash explained to his students that *"Love your neighbor as yourself"* means you must always assume that your neighbor is as complicated as you.

A student inquired, "So that means that instead of doing homework when he was a kid, my sixty-six-year-old neighbor wept with awe over Elvis Presley's cover of "A Fool Such As I" that made Bill Haley's version pale like an American flat 'r' in *rosh* against an Israeli smooth authentic growl? And he bought the Elvis record with bar mitzvah money he'd secretly planned to spend on Cavalier cigarettes?"

The Razbash replied, "Yes, my beloved smarty pants. That's exactly what I mean."

God's Inventions

God invented the Christian to teach Midrash without a wink.
God invented the Pagan to teach we have a fighting chance to lose.
God invented the Scientist to teach all places—*ha-makom*—are One.
God invented the Tyrant to teach not everyone chosen has Torah.
God invented the Israeli to teach the rewards of settling for less.

God invented the Harlot to teach love without love is honesty.
God invented the Artist to teach sex without sex is beauty.
God invented Yeats to teach 'Bodily decrepitude is wisdom.'
God invented Woman to teach every creature on earth how to pray.
God invented Herself to teach unabashed affection for men.

Against Santayana

The Razbash disagrees. "History is the enemy.

What we learn from slavery is that it's possible. Here's how. . .
What we learn from genocide is that it's possible. Here's how. . .

Do you want to prevent future tyrants? Make them think they're the first.
Lonely explorers are easily daunted. Ignorance is our last best hope.

And do you want young believers to keep their faith?
Don't tell them about their fathers."

Treasure Maps

Let's agree that the events in the Bible
can be placed in one-to-one correspondence
with evolution, ancient history, and Big Bang cosmology.

Let's agree that all the character traits in astrology
can be placed in one-to-one correspondence
with character traits in a recent psychology book.

Let's agree that all the diseases we'll ever get,
avoid, spread, or read about
can be accounted for in our DNA.

Let's agree these all are treasure maps.
Now let's find the treasure.

Why the Good Must Suffer for the Bad

Why must good people suffer for bad people?
Because that's the meaning of *bad*:
to cause the *good* to suffer for you.

And the meaning of good is to suffer
for the undeserving bad.
We good people need bad people

more than they need us.
Without them we would not be good,
but without us they would be just as bad.

Old Age

—*Mishnah Sanhedrin 4:9*

The Razbash asks, "Why does it read 'an *entire* world'?
Why not simply 'world'?"

When you die,
everything you learned
searches for a new learner,
but everything you did not learn
ceases to exist for eternity.

That is why it is incumbent
to learn as much as you can,
even in old age, until your last breath.
The *entire* world needs you.

The Razbash Blesses a Marriage

May you keep it precious like the vowels from a language teacher's lips
and keep it tasty like a server's busy garlic fingertips.

May you keep it subtle like the balance of compliant springs in bed
and keep it private like the photos of the ones you did not wed.

May you keep it supple like *tefillin* as they bind along the arm
and keep it formal when you understand that you can do real harm.

The Four Children Answer The Four Questions

1.

The *wise* child answers the question about *matzah*.
It is restrained bread. She knows not to be reckless.
Freedom is a well-wrought *matzah* of obedient self-control.

2.

It is *wicked* to be casual about freedom.
Insouciant, indifferent, *reclining,* blasé,
wicked children slouch with clever questions,
treating freedom like ordinary air.

3.

Because he mistakes the hidden for the missing,
the *simple* child answers the *dunking* question.
That which is below the surface vanishes from his mind.
Submerged, it never was. We dunk twice to expose his mistake.

4.

The child who *does not know to ask* knows only *bitter herbs.*
His questioning lips taste festering yogurt,
forgotten in a high school gym, lost to bad advice.

Holocaust

On Yom HaShoah, The Razbash recites this poem.

Unmarried brilliant middle-aged woman
following the Mets in your New York City flat,
your walls are lined with college books,
Hundertwasser posters,
and a farewell card from 'all the crazy folks at'
that ad agency you worked for once
before you studied law.

Year after year, a new Bloomingdale's calendar
shines on your closet door.
Year after year, your husband's mother dies
naked, choking, crowded, gassed
before your husband is born.
They poisoned our imagination
for a thousand years.

~~~~~~~~~~~~~~~~~~~~~~~~~~~~

Rabbi Moshe asks,
"It's Hitler's fault she can't find a husband?"
Rabbi Avram answers,
"They poisoned our imagination for a thousand years."

God Explains Death

This is the only time The Razbash claims to have spoken with God.

God explained, "Remember when you moved
from town to town when you were little?
Well, that's what death is like.
You will have to learn a different grading system
and practice names of new friends.
You will feel like a spy, trust no one, and know it.
But I will be with you the whole time.
For the first few months every night
you will clutch your radio under the covers,
seeking signals from the towns you left behind.
You have known death all your life, but this time
it will not go away."

The twelve-year-old Razbash asked, "Will I have girlfriends?"

God replied, "I don't think you understand your question."

Acts of Love

Teaching is an act of love:
Why else share what you know?
Writing is an act of love:
Why else make it clear to strangers?

Dignity is an act of love:
Why else keep pain to yourself?
Imagination is an act of love:
Why else does the real world matter?

A Disciple Remembers

1.

I was playing backgammon with two Arabs in their twenties
while their teenage brother watched from a distance, smiling.
After I lost to each brother, I challenged the silent one.
He smiled but stayed in his seat. I repeated the offer in English.
"You don't want to play him," the brothers said with reverence.
Years later I reported this to the Razbash. He suggested that
their young brother was learning disabled.

2.

I was a kibbutz volunteer sorting eggplant from a conveyor belt,
whistling American and Israeli songs with anyone who would join in.
In the middle of my concert the branch coordinator announced a break
for the rest of the day. The next morning I was assigned to work in the kitchen.
Years later I reported this to the Razbash. He told me I had been fired.

Tell It to the Lamb

I was pouring concrete near the kibbutz dining room
when a hired hand I'd worked with the day before
asked me to hold the legs of a whimpering lamb.
I obeyed, and he cut the lamb's throat.
After blood seeped onto the grass, he separated flesh from fur.
I pictured the lamb chops Mother made when I was four.

Instead of dinner that night,
I wrote a long letter to The Razbash about how at last
I understood temple rites and why the Hebrew root word
for *sacrifice* and *near* are the same.
I held forth about how physical sacrifice makes elusive life
tangible, subordinate, close, and holy. It begins with awe,
then falls into technical procedures, necessary distancing rituals.
I quoted him his own saying,
Religion begins in poetry and ends in bureaucracy.
I mused on my unconscious juxtaposition of savagery and ecstasy
with precious childhood memories, and concluded with a prayer-poem
that the temple be rebuilt, but that instead of sacrificing animals,
we sacrifice nationalism, narcissism, chauvinism, and ourselves.
I closed with a heartrending rhetorical question:
Isn't that what the *Aleinu* for our time is all about?

Three days later I received a postcard from The Razbash
with this five-word reply: "Tell it to the lamb."

About the Author

Zev Shanken lives in Teaneck, New Jersey, and currently teaches English at Kean College and the College of Staten Island. He taught for many years in the New York City school system. He is a co-curator of a poetry reading series in Bergen Country, New Jersey, and serves on the steering committee of *brevitas*, a writers' group dedicated to the short poem. His chapbook, *Al Het*, is available from Blue Begonia Press.